SUSAN MARINACCIO

The Construction Accountant's Toolbox

The Growth Guide for Controllers, Bookkeepers, and the Construction Companies That Depend on Them.

First published by Susan Marinaccio 2026

"Three free Excel tools are available for download at www.constructionaccountantstoolbox.com — the Companion Workbook with eight calculation tabs and a full glossary of construction accounting terms used throughout this book, the Example Dashboard pre-filled with sample data, and the Blank Dashboard ready for your own numbers. No email required."

First edition

ISBN (paperback): 979-8-9959482-1-6
ISBN (hardcover): 979-8-9959482-0-9

This book was professionally typeset on Reedsy.
Find out more at reedsy.com

Contents

Title Page

The Growth Guide for Controllers, Bookkeepers, and the Construction Companies That Depend on Them

Susan Marinaccio

Construction Financial Strategist

For permission requests, contact the author at:

www.constructionaccountantstoolbox.com

Three free Excel tools are available for download at www.constructionaccountantstoolbox.com — the Companion Workbook with eight calculation tabs, the Example Dashboard pre-filled with sample data, and the Blank Dashboard ready for your own numbers. No email required.

First Edition, 2026

Published in the United States of America

ISBN: 979-8-9959482-1-6 Paperback

ISBN: 979-8-9959482-0-9 Hardcover

DISCLAIMER

The information contained in this book is for educational and informational purposes only. It is designed to provide practical guidance to controllers, bookkeepers, and owners of small to mid-size construction companies based on the author's professional experience.

This book does not constitute accounting, legal, tax, or financial advice. The examples, calculations, and case scenarios presented are illustrative in nature and are intended to demonstrate general principles. They may not reflect the specific circumstances of your company, your state, or your industry.

Every construction company is unique. Labor burden rates, tax rates, insurance costs, overhead structures, and financial requirements vary significantly by company size, trade, geography, and individual circumstance. The figures used in examples throughout this book are estimates used for educational purposes only and should not be applied directly to your business without independent verification.

Readers are strongly encouraged to consult with a licensed CPA, attorney,

Acknowledgments

There are people without whom this book would not exist — not because they wrote it, but because they made it possible for me to.

To God — for the clarity to see what I was capable of and the strength to see it through.

To my husband Steve — thank you for being my biggest believer, for your patience with a wife so often lost in thought, and for believing in me every time I needed to step outside my comfort zone.

To my family — for every evening I was at my desk instead of at the table, for every moment of patience you gave me without being asked, and for believing in this before I had the words to explain what it was going to be. You are the reason any of this matters.

For this season in my career — and in my life — I want to thank A-Christian Glass & Mirror Co. Ron and Stacie, your belief in me made this possible. You gave me the trust, the support, and the environment to grow fully into my craft. You gave me the freedom to make change and the space to find my voice. None of this would exist without God's hand guiding the path — and without Ron taking a chance on me. From the bottom of my heart, thank you.

To everyone who showed up in the comments, joined the community, reached out to ask when the book was coming — you reminded me on the hard days that this work was worth finishing.

This book was built from nothing. It exists because of you.

Built, Not Taught

I did not start with a finance degree, a CPA firm behind me, or a corporate accounting team.

I started with responsibility.

Responsibility to keep the doors open. Responsibility to make payroll. Responsibility to make sure the numbers were right — even when I did not fully understand them yet.

There was no high-end advisor guiding every move. There was no team of analysts building reports. There was work. There were problems. There were limited resources. And there was a business that needed structure.

So I learned.
Not in a classroom.
In real time.

I learned because I had to. I learned what happens when job costs are not tracked properly. I learned what happens when overhead is not understood. I learned how quickly cash disappears when financial structure is weak. I learned that revenue does not equal profit. And I learned that most construction companies are not failing because they lack work — they are failing because they lack financial clarity.

This book is not written for the $50-million contractor with a CFO and a national CPA firm.

This book is written for:

- The small to mid-sized general contractor
- The subcontractor who grew faster than their systems
- The owner who is excellent in the field but unsure in the financials
- The conscientious bookkeeper who wants to become more
- The controller who learned by doing

Most small construction businesses operate with limited capital. They cannot afford high-end advisory teams, highly skilled accounting departments, or layers of financial management.

What they can afford is discipline.
What they can build is structure.
And what they need is understanding.

You do not need to be a CPA to build a financially strong construction company. You need to understand how the numbers connect — what the owner truly needs to see, how to protect cash, how to measure real profitability, and how to turn reporting into decision-making.

The Construction Accountant's Toolbox is not about bookkeeping. It is about building strength.

This book will teach mechanics. But more importantly, it will teach interpretation. Because numbers alone do not build companies. Understanding does.

If you are conscientious, willing to learn, and ready to step into a larger role

— this book is for you.

You do not need to start with everything.

You can build it.

I did.

And so can you.

The Construction Controller: Builder of Financial Strength

Most small construction companies do not start with a controller. They start with a bookkeeper. Someone who pays the bills, reconciles the bank, processes payroll, and keeps things moving.

That is necessary.
But it is not enough.

Bookkeeping records history. A controller builds the future.

A bookkeeper asks: was this entered correctly? A controller asks: what does this mean for the business? That difference changes everything. In construction, margins are tight. Cash flow is unpredictable. Projects overlap. Costs move before revenue is collected. If someone in the organization is not interpreting the numbers, the company is operating blind. And blind companies grow fast — right into failure.

The Controller Is the Bridge

In small construction companies there is usually a disconnect. The field speaks production. The owner speaks sales. The office speaks transactions. The controller must speak all three. You must understand how a job is bid, how it is built, how it is billed, how it is paid, and how it affects cash. Without that understanding, financial reports are just paper. With it, they become protection.

The Protector of Cash

Most small construction companies fail for one reason: cash mismanagement. Not lack of work. Not lack of skill. The controller must know what cash is committed but not yet spent, what revenue is earned but not yet billed, what is sitting in retainage, what overhead must be covered monthly, and what the draw schedule timing looks like. The owner often focuses on the next job. The controller focuses on survival. That balance keeps the company standing.

The Educator to the Owner

Many construction owners are excellent builders. But they were never taught how to read Work in Progress reports, gross profit by division, labor burden percentages, overhead absorption, or true net operating income. The controller must translate. Not overwhelm. Not criticize. Translate. You are not there to prove intelligence. You are there to create clarity. When an owner understands the numbers, decision-making improves. And when decision-making improves, profit follows.

The Early Warning System

A strong controller sees problems before they explode. You see margin erosion, cost overruns, labor inefficiencies, unbalanced overhead, and cash gaps forming. You are not reacting to failure. You are preventing it. This is not about being dramatic. It is about being disciplined.

Built, Not Born

Most controllers in small construction companies did not start as controllers. They started as administrative assistants, bookkeepers, payroll clerks, or office managers. They learned because they had to. They stayed late. They asked questions. They fixed mistakes. They rebuilt systems. They grew into the role. If that is you, understand this: you do not need a CPA license to think strategically. You need curiosity, discipline, consistency, and a willingness to learn.

Skill compounds. Just like profit does.

How This Builds the Business Stronger

When a controller moves from maintenance to strategy, bids improve, margins stabilize, cash flow becomes predictable, banks gain confidence, bonding capacity increases, and owners sleep better. Financial strength is not luck. It is built. And the controller is one of the primary builders.

Tool #1

The Financial Blueprint: Your Chart of Accounts

You cannot build strength on a weak foundation.

Most small construction companies do not design their Chart of Accounts. They inherit it — from a prior bookkeeper, a CPA who set it up for taxes, a QuickBooks default template, or how we have always done it. And then they wonder why their financials do not make sense. If your Chart of Accounts is wrong, every report that comes out of it will mislead you.

What a Properly Built COA Must Answer

Your Chart of Accounts is not just a list of categories. It is the structure that determines how profit is measured, how overhead is separated, how job costs are tracked, how divisions are evaluated, and how cash flow is understood. It must be able to answer five critical questions quickly:

- What did we earn?
- What did it cost to earn it?
- What is true gross profit?
- What does it cost to operate each division?
- What is real net operating income?

If your P&L cannot answer those five without explanation, the structure is

wrong.

Why Small Construction Companies Get This Wrong

Because they set it up for compliance, not control. Tax reporting is not the same as operational reporting. A CPA's job is to file accurately. A controller's job is to build clarity. Those are different missions. Most small businesses have one revenue account, a large job materials bucket, no labor burden separation, overhead buried inside cost of goods sold, no division visibility, and owner activity mixed into operating expenses. That structure hides reality. And hidden reality destroys margin.

Case Example: The Illusion of Profit

Real-World Scenario

A small GC generates $2,000,000 in revenue. The owner reviews the P&L and sees $600,000 in gross profit. He feels strong. Bonuses are discussed. Maybe a new truck.

But the bookkeeper has been coding office payroll, vehicle expenses, insurance, software subscriptions, and rent directly into job costs — treating them as direct expenses tied to the work rather than overhead that exists regardless of how many jobs are running.

Here is what the P&L actually looks like before the restructure - with the $480,000 in overhead costs misclassified as direct job costs, the gross profit reported to the owner is nowhere near what the company is actually earning:

Before COA Restructure

Account	Amount
Revenue	$2,000,000
Direct Job Costs (Including $480,000 misclassified overhead)	$1,880,000
Gross Profit	$120,000
Overhead	$0
Net Income	$120,000
Gross Margin	6%

The owner is only seeing $120,000 in gross profit — because $480,000 in overhead is buried inside his job costs, making his jobs look far more expensive than they are. He has no idea what it costs to run his company independent of the jobs. Every decision he makes is built on incomplete information.

When the COA is restructured correctly and the $480,000 in overhead costs are moved out of direct job costs and into the proper 7000 section where they belong, the P&L tells a completely different story:

After COA Restructure

Account	Amount
Revenue	$2,000,000
Direct Job Costs	$1,400,000
Gross Profit	$600,000
Overhead	$480,000
Net Income	$120,000
Gross Margin	30%

The net income is identical. Not a single dollar changed hands. But everything else did.

Now the owner can see that his true gross margin is 30%. His jobs are actually performing well. The problem is not the work. It is the overhead load — and now he can see it, measure it, and manage it.

More importantly he can now have the right conversation. At 30% gross margin and $480,000 in annual overhead his monthly break-even is $133,333 in revenue. He is covering it comfortably at $2,000,000 annually. He has $120,000 in net income.

The truck? He can afford it — if he finances it carefully and keeps the overhead line from growing faster than revenue.

Before the restructure that conversation was impossible. The gross profit was buried inside job costs. The overhead was invisible. And every decision the owner made was based on numbers that were telling the wrong story.

Structure does not change the money. It reveals where it actually went.

And once you can see it clearly — you can manage it.

Structure matters.

The Three-Tier Structure: How the COA Should Be Built

A properly structured construction COA has three distinct tiers. Most companies have two. That missing tier is where clarity goes to die.

Tier 1 — Direct Job Costs (5000 section)

Everything directly attributable to a specific project. Labor, burden, materials, subcontractors, other, and equipment rental. These costs live and die with the job.

Tier 2 — Department Indirect Costs (6000 section)

Costs that belong to a specific department or division — Commercial, Residential, Service — but cannot be tied to a single job. They exist because the department exists. Examples include a division superintendent's salary, a department-specific vehicle, or tools maintained for a division's use. When you run a department-level P&L these costs appear under that department, giving you a true picture of what it costs to operate each division. What remains after the 6000 section is each department's contribution toward company overhead.

Tier 3 — Company Overhead (7000 section of the general ledger)

True company-wide costs that exist regardless of how many divisions you run or how many jobs are active. Office rent, executive salaries, company-wide insurance, marketing, software, accounting fees. These belong to the company — not to any single department. Only a portion of these costs can be allocated to departments or projects. More on that in Tool #5.

The Construction COA Blueprint

REVENUE

4000 — Revenue

- 4010 — Commercial Contract Revenue
- 4020 — Residential Contract Revenue

• 4030 — Service Revenue

DIRECT JOB COSTS — 5000 section

5000 — Direct Job Costs

• 5010 — Labor

• 5020 — Materials

• 5030 — Equipment Rental

• 5040 — Subcontractors

• 5050 — Other Direct Job Costs

DEPARTMENT INDIRECT COSTS — 6000 section (by division)

6000 — Department Indirect Costs

Commercial Division:

• 6010 — Commercial Division Supervision Salaries

• 6020 — Commercial Division Vehicles

• 6030 — Commercial Division Small Tools and Equipment

• 6040 — Commercial Division Miscellaneous Materials

Residential Division:

• 6100 — Residential Division Supervision Salaries

• 6110 — Residential Division Vehicles

• 6120 — Residential Division Small Tools and Equipment

• 6130 — Residential Division Miscellaneous Materials

COMPANY OVERHEAD — 7000 section of the General Ledger

7000 — Company Overhead

• 7010 — Office Payroll

• 7020 — Executive Compensation

• 7030 — Office Rent and Utilities

• 7040 — Company Insurance

• 7050 — Marketing and Advertising

• 7060 — Software and Technology

• 7070 — Professional Fees (CPA, Legal)

• 7080 — General Vehicle Expenses

• 7090 — Miscellaneous Administrative

OTHER INCOME AND OWNER ACTIVITY

These items do not belong in operating accounts. They live below net operating income and are found on specific financial reports as noted.

· **Interest Income / Interest Expense** — *(Income Statement — below operating income; also Balance Sheet if accrued)*

· **Owner Loans** — *(Balance Sheet — shown as a liability (loans from owner) or asset (loans to owner))*

· **Owner Distributions** — *(Balance Sheet — shown as a reduction to equity in the equity section)*

· **Intercompany Transactions** — *(Balance Sheet and Income Statement —* ***must be tracked separately by entity and eliminated in consolidated reporting)***

Note: Each of these items — interest income and expense, owner loans, owner distributions, and intercompany transactions — is addressed in context throughout the tools that follow. Owner distributions and equity treatment are covered in Tool #1B. WIP-related contract assets and liabilities are addressed in Tool #3. When in doubt, consult your CPA for entity-specific guidance on intercompany transactions and loan structuring.

You cannot scale chaos. You can scale clarity.

How This Builds the Business Stronger

When your Chart of Accounts is structured properly, gross profit becomes real, overhead becomes measurable, each division can be evaluated on its own performance, pricing improves, cash planning improves, banks gain confidence, and owners stop guessing. Division-level P&Ls become possible — and those reports will show you which part of your business is carrying the company and which part needs attention.

Controller Action Steps

Download the free Excel worksheets at www.constructionaccountantstoolbox.com.

1. Review every revenue account — is it lumped together or separated by department?
2. Ensure labor burden is included in your job budgets alongside base labor.

The full burden calculation — what it includes, how to calculate your rate, and how to apply it — is covered in detail in Tool #2.

3. Identify which costs belong in the 6000 section as department indirect — move them out of direct job costs and into the correct division account.
4. Identify which costs belong in the 7000 section as company overhead — move them out of both direct job costs and department indirect and into the overhead section where they belong.
5. Ensure owner distributions and intercompany activity are not buried in operating expenses.
6. Confirm division tracking exists for every department you operate.

Do not overhaul everything overnight. Begin restructuring intentionally and consistently. Every improvement strengthens the foundation.

Tool #1B

The Balance Sheet Blueprint

This tool is labeled #1B rather than #2 because the Balance Sheet is the other half of the foundation the Chart of Accounts starts — the two must be built together.

The Chart of Accounts tells you how to organize your financial information. This tool is labeled #1B rather than #2 because the Balance Sheet is the other half of the foundation the Chart of Accounts starts — the two must be built together.

The income statement tells you whether you made money. But the balance sheet tells you what the company actually is — what it owns, what it owes, and what is left over for the owner. In small construction companies the balance sheet is often the most overlooked financial report. That is a mistake. Because the balance sheet does not just reflect performance. It reflects reality.

A properly maintained balance sheet is also what your bank examines when you apply for a line of credit. What your bonding company reviews when assessing capacity. What a buyer evaluates if you ever sell the business. It is the financial foundation of the company — and it needs to be accurate.

The income statement tells you how the year went. The balance sheet tells you where the company stands.

The Three-Part Structure

The balance sheet is built on one simple equation that never changes:

Assets = Liabilities + Owner Equity

What the company owns equals what it owes plus what belongs to the owner. This is why it is called a balance sheet — because the two sides always balance. The total of all assets will always equal the total of all liabilities plus the total of all equity. Always. If it does not balance, something has been posted incorrectly. Every transaction that touches the balance sheet preserves this equation. Every time. No exceptions.

Part One — Assets: What the Company Owns

Assets are everything of value the company holds. In construction they fall into two categories — current assets that move within the year, and long-term assets that hold value over time.

Current Assets

• Cash — what is in the bank accounts right now. This is the most liquid asset and the one the owner watches most closely. It is also the most misleading if you are not reconciling it against your WIP schedule monthly.

• Accounts Receivable — money earned and billed but not yet collected. These are invoices sent to clients or GCs that are outstanding. Age this balance every month. Anything over 90 days needs a conversation.

• retainage receivable — money earned and withheld by the client throughout the life of a job. This is a genuine asset — you have earned it — but you cannot touch it until the job is complete and accepted. Track it separately from regular accounts receivable so you always know exactly what is held and when it is expected to release.

• Inventory — materials purchased and on hand but not yet assigned to a job. Not all construction companies carry inventory but if yours does it belongs here as an asset until it is consumed on a project.

• Prepaid Expenses — costs paid in advance for future periods. The most common example in construction is insurance premiums paid upfront and amortized monthly. The unamortized balance sits here as a current asset until it is expensed. See Tool #6 for the monthly journal entry.

• WIP Adjustment — Contract Assets and Contract Liabilities — this is where your WIP schedule connects directly to the balance sheet. If your jobs are underbilled — you have earned more than you have invoiced — the difference is a contract asset. If your jobs are overbilled — you have invoiced more than you have earned — the difference is a contract liability. These are not opinions. They are journal entries that must be made at every close to keep your balance sheet accurate. See Tool #3 for the full mechanics. And keep this in mind: if you have not earned it, you cannot represent it as revenue. The journal entry either increases or decreases your recognized revenue based on whether you are over or underbilled. This is not optional — it is a GAAP requirement under ASC 606. (ASC stands for Accounting Standards Codification — the official numbered rulebook for U.S. accounting standards. When you see ASC followed by a number throughout this book, it is simply a reference to the specific rule that applies.)

Long-Term Assets

• Equipment and Vehicles — any piece of equipment or vehicle owned by the company is recorded here at its original purchase cost. This includes trucks, trailers, heavy equipment, and company-owned tools above your capitalization threshold.

• Accumulated Depreciation — a contra-asset account that reduces the book value of your equipment over time. Your CPA will calculate and post the annual depreciation journal entries. Do not skip this. Depreciation is not just a tax strategy — it is the accounting recognition that assets lose value as they age and are used. Your net equipment value on the balance sheet is original cost minus accumulated depreciation.

Always work with your CPA on annual depreciation journal entries for fixed assets. The method used — straight-line, accelerated, section 179 — affects both your balance sheet and your tax return and should be applied consistently year over year.

Part Two — Liabilities: What the Company Owes

Liabilities are everything the company is obligated to pay. Like assets they are split into current obligations due within the year and long-term obligations that extend beyond it.

Current Liabilities

• Accounts Payable — money owed to vendors and suppliers for materials, services, and expenses already received but not yet paid. Keep this current. Aging payables damage vendor relationships and credit terms.

• Credit Cards — balances on company credit cards are a liability. They belong here — not buried in expense accounts — so the full picture of what the company owes is visible on one report.

• Payroll Liabilities — taxes withheld from employee paychecks and employer payroll taxes that have been accrued but not yet remitted to the government. This balance should clear every pay period. If it is growing something is wrong.

• Retainage Payable — money you are holding back from your subcontractors, mirroring what the GC or client is holding from you. This is a liability because you owe it to your subs when the work is complete and accepted. Track it by subcontractor so you know exactly what you will need to release at each job closeout.

• Line of Credit — the outstanding balance on any revolving credit facility. This is a current liability because it is typically callable and renewed annually. Monitor it monthly against your cash forecast.

• Contract Liabilities — overbilled amounts from your WIP schedule. Money collected from clients for work not yet performed. This is not profit. It must be protected and tracked separately every single month.

Long-Term Liabilities

• Equipment Loans — financed equipment creates a long-term liability on the balance sheet. The principal balance outstanding is recorded here and reduces as payments are made. The interest portion of each payment goes to the income statement as an interest expense — it does not reduce the loan balance.

• Vehicle Loans — same treatment as equipment loans. Each vehicle financed carries its own loan balance tracked here against the asset on the other side.

• Building or Construction Loans — if the company owns real property with a mortgage or has a construction loan outstanding it lives here as a long-term liability with the corresponding asset on the other side of the balance sheet.

Part Three — Owner Equity: What the Owner Actually Owns

Owner equity is the value left after all debts are paid. Rearranging the same equation: Assets minus Liabilities equals Equity. It is what the owner actually owns — the net worth of the business after every obligation is satisfied. Equity tells the real story of whether the company is building something of lasting value or slowly being hollowed out by debt and distributions.

- Owner's Capital — the money the owner originally invested in the business to get it started or to fund its growth over time. This is the owner's direct financial stake — the amount they put in with their own hands.
- Retained Earnings — the accumulated profits the company has kept over its lifetime instead of distributing them to the owner. Every year that the company earns a profit and does not distribute all of it, the remainder stays in the business as retained earnings. This is the financial reservoir that gives the company strength over time. A company with strong retained earnings is a company that has been building — not just surviving.
- Current Year Net Income — the profit or loss from the current operating year flows from the income statement into equity. A profitable year increases equity. A loss year reduces it.
- Owner Draws and Distributions — when the owner takes money out of the business it reduces equity. Distributions are not an expense on the income statement. They are a reduction of equity on the balance sheet. This distinction matters because distributions do not reduce taxable income — they reduce the owner's stake in the company.
- Owner Loans — if the owner has loaned money to the company it appears as a liability. If the company has loaned money to the owner it appears as an asset. Either way it must be tracked separately and clearly — mixing owner loan activity into operating accounts distorts every financial report the company produces.

A growing equity balance over time means the company is building real value. A shrinking equity balance — especially one driven by distributions exceeding net income — is a warning sign that needs to be put in front of the owner clearly and without delay.

Case Example — The Balance Sheet Nobody Read

Real-World Scenario

A small GC had been profitable on paper for three consecutive years. The owner felt strong. Revenue was growing. But nobody was reading the balance sheet. Accounts receivable had aged significantly with two large clients consistently paying at 90 days. retainage receivable was growing faster than retainage was being released. Equipment loans had been refinanced and extended. And owner distributions over the three years had exceeded net income. Equity was negative. The company owed more than it owned. The income statement said profitable. The balance sheet said insolvent. The income statement was not lying. The balance sheet was just not being read.

How This Builds the Business Stronger

When the balance sheet is maintained accurately and reviewed monthly, the owner sees the company's true financial position — not just the month's performance. Banks and bonding companies gain confidence because your numbers are clean and reconciled. Distribution decisions become grounded in equity reality rather than cash balance. And the controller becomes the person in the room who can answer the hardest question any owner faces: are we actually building something, or are we just staying busy?

Controller Action Steps

Download the free Excel worksheets at www.constructionaccountantstoolbox.com.

• Reconcile your bank accounts every month without exception — the cash balance on the balance sheet must match your bank statement.

• Age your accounts receivable monthly — flag anything over 60 days and bring it to ownership.

• Track retainage receivable separately from accounts receivable — know the balance, the job it belongs to, and the expected release date.

• Post WIP journal entries every month — contract assets for underbillings, contract liabilities for overbillings. If you have not earned it, you cannot represent it.

• Reconcile retainage payable to your subcontractor records every quarter — know exactly what you owe each sub at job closeout.

• Review owner equity monthly — compare distributions to net income and flag any quarter where distributions are outpacing earnings.

• Ensure owner loans and owner draws are recorded in the correct equity or liability accounts — never buried in operating expenses.

• Work with your CPA on annual depreciation journal entries for all fixed assets — and update your asset schedule every time equipment is purchased or disposed of.

• Bring the balance sheet to every ownership meeting alongside the income statement. One report tells you how you performed. The other tells you what you are worth.

Tool #2

Job Costing: The Truth Serum

If the Chart of Accounts is the blueprint, job costing is the diagnostic scan. It tells you the truth — whether you are ready to hear it or not.

Most construction companies think they know if a job made money. They do not. They know if cash came in. They know if the job felt busy. They know if the client was satisfied.

That is not the same as profitability.
Job costing removes opinion.
It replaces it with measurement.

The Five Direct Cost Categories

Before a single cost can be tracked accurately, you need to understand where it belongs. Every cost on a construction job fits into one of five categories — and each category maps directly to a sub-account under your Direct Job Costs account (5000) on the Chart of Accounts. These are not standalone accounts; they are the numbered sub-accounts that sit beneath the 5000 parent. No exceptions. No gray areas.

Labor — 5010

Labor is the wages paid to your field employees for time worked on a specific job. Nothing more, nothing less. If an employee works Tuesday through

Thursday on one job and Friday on another, the hours split between those jobs accordingly. Labor follows the worker, and the worker follows the job. Labor burden — the employer payroll taxes, workers compensation, general liability tied to field payroll, health insurance, benefits, and PTO that sit on top of base wages — represents the true cost of employment. These are not estimates. They are actual expenses that hit real general ledger accounts when payroll is run. Burden must be included in every job budget alongside base labor — because if you only budget the wage, you are undercounting the true cost of every hour worked. Most accounting software will ask you for a burden percentage. Once configured, it calculates and posts burden automatically each time payroll is processed, distributing those costs to the correct accounts alongside labor.

The critical discipline: labor must be coded to the correct job at the time it is posted — not at month end in a bulk entry. Miscoded labor quietly destroys the accuracy of every job cost report downstream.

Materials — 5020

Materials are physical items purchased for a job that are incorporated into the finished work and remain at the job when the project is complete. Lumber. Concrete. Drywall. Electrical wire. Pipe. Fixtures. If you buy it for a job and it stays in the building when you leave — it is a material. When a material invoice arrives it must be coded to the specific job it was purchased for. One purchase order covering materials for three jobs must be split accordingly.

Equipment Rental — 5030

Equipment rental covers the cost of construction machinery hired specifically for a project. Excavators. Lifts. Cranes. Scaffolding. If you rent equipment for a job, the rental invoice is a direct job cost coded to that job. Company-owned equipment is handled differently — it is depreciated as an asset on the balance sheet. If financed, the loan is a liability and the payments reduce that liability over time. For the small to mid-sized GC or subcontractor, building internal equipment allocation rates for owned equipment adds administrative burden without proportional benefit. Keep it simple: the 5030 account is for rental equipment on specific jobs.

Subcontractors — 5040

Subcontractors are outside companies or individuals hired to perform a specific scope of work. Your electrical sub. Your HVAC contractor. Your concrete crew. A single subcontractor often works on multiple jobs simultaneously and sends one invoice covering work across several projects. That invoice cannot go to a general subcontractor account. It must be split and allocated to each job based on work performed. This requires communication between the controller and the project manager — and it requires the PM to document what work was completed on each job during the billing period.

Other Direct Job Costs — 5050

Other captures job-related costs that are consumed in the process of completing the work but are not physically incorporated into the finished product and do not remain at the job when you leave. Fuel used by equipment operating on a specific job. Job-site consumables such as drill bits, saw blades, sandpaper, caulk. Temporary materials used during construction and removed at completion. Small tools purchased specifically for a job and consumed in the process. Job-specific dump fees and waste disposal. The test for Other is straightforward: was this cost incurred specifically because of this job and was it consumed or used up in the process? If yes — it belongs in Other, coded to that job.

Phase Codes: The Language of Job Costing

Before costs can be tracked by category, everyone in the company must speak the same language. That language is phase codes. A phase code is a simple numbered identifier assigned to a specific type of work on a project. When a field employee codes their time, when a material invoice comes in, when a subcontractor bill is posted — the phase code tells the system exactly what part of the job that cost belongs to.

Without phase codes, all your job costs pile into one bucket. You know what the job cost in total. You do not know what it cost to frame it or finish it or run the electrical. And that means you cannot improve your next bid. You are guessing forward based on total numbers instead of learning from the detail.

Here is a practical standard phase code list for a commercial GC. Adapt it to your trade. Eliminate what does not apply. Add what is specific to your work. But keep it short enough that your crew can use it consistently.

- 01 — General Conditions: Project management, superintendent time, site setup, permits, inspections, temporary facilities
- 02 — Site Work and Demolition: Excavation, grading, demolition, site utilities, paving
- 03 — Concrete: Footings, foundations, slabs, flatwork
- 04 — Masonry: Block, brick, stone, mortar work
- 05 — Structural Steel and Framing: Steel erection, metal framing, miscellaneous metals
- 06 — Rough Carpentry: Wood framing, sheathing, blocking, rough lumber
- 07 — Roofing and Waterproofing: Roofing systems, flashing, waterproofing, insulation
- 08 — Doors, Windows and Glazing: Door and frame installation, hardware, windows, storefront
- 09 — Finishes: Drywall, taping, painting, flooring, ceilings, tile, millwork
- 10 — Specialties: Signage, toilet accessories, fire extinguishers, anything not in another phase
- 11 — Plumbing: All plumbing rough and finish work
- 12 — HVAC: Heating, ventilation, air conditioning, sheet metal
- 13 — Electrical: All electrical rough and finish, low voltage, fire alarm, data
- 14 — Equipment Rental: Rented equipment specific to the job
- 15 — Subcontractors Other: Any subcontracted scope not captured in trade phases above
- 16 — Change Orders: All costs related to approved change orders, tracked

separately from original scope

*The phase codes above are a practical field-ready simplification designed for small to mid-size construction companies. For a complete and trade-specific code structure, refer to the **CSI MasterFormat** — the industry standard division and section numbering system published by the Construction Specifications Institute. MasterFormat divisions can be viewed and downloaded at **csinet.org**. Codes are organized by construction type and trade, allowing you to build a phase code list tailored precisely to your company's scope of work.*

One system. Every job. Every person. Every time. Consistency is what makes the data trustworthy. And trustworthy data is what builds a stronger company.

Labor Burden: The Hidden Margin Erosion

If you apply only the hourly wage to jobs, you are undercosting every hour of field labor. Labor burden is the real cost of employment that sits on top of base wages — employer payroll taxes (FICA, FUTA, SUTA), workers compensation, a portion of general liability insurance attributable to field payroll, health insurance, benefits, 401(k) match, and PTO. These are not estimates or adjustments. They are actual expenses that hit real general ledger accounts when payroll is run. Ignoring burden creates false gross profit — and false gross profit leads to underpricing future work.

A note on general liability in the burden calculation: your GL premium is rated on gross revenue, but the underlying exposure is driven by the work your field crews perform. The portion of the GL premium attributable to field operations can reasonably be included in your burden rate. Work with your broker or CPA to determine the appropriate allocation — typically derived from your audit worksheets or trade classification codes.

What Labor Burden Actually Looks Like in Numbers

A field laborer earns $28.00 per hour. That is what shows on the timecard. That is not what that employee costs the company.

Here is what the true hourly cost looks like:

- Base Wage: $28.00
- Federal Payroll Taxes — FICA (Social Security + Medicare) 7.65%: $2.14
- Federal Unemployment — FUTA approx 0.6%: $0.17
- State Unemployment — SUTA varies, estimate 2.5%: $0.70
- Workers Compensation — varies by trade, estimate 12%: $3.36
- General Liability — estimate 3% of wage: $0.84
- PTO and Holiday Pay — estimate 5% of wage: $1.40

Total Burden Cost per Hour: $8.61
True Hourly Cost: $36.61
Burden Rate: approximately 31%

Note on benefits: Health insurance, benefits, and any 401(k) match are not included in this example because they vary significantly by company. If your company offers these benefits, add your actual per-employee cost per hour to arrive at your true burden rate. For a company providing health coverage, the total burden rate commonly reaches 35% to 45% or higher.

Now apply that to a job. If you estimate 500 field labor hours on a project at $28.00 per hour, your labor budget is $14,000. But your true labor cost is $18,305. That is a $4,305 gap on a single line item on a single job. Multiply that across every job in a busy year and you understand exactly where the margin went.

The burden rate varies by company, by trade, and by state. Workers compensation alone can range from 5% for lower-risk trades to 25% or higher for structural and roofing work. The construction industry average burden rate typically falls between 20% and 40% of direct labor cost. Calculate your own rate using your actual payroll tax filings, your workers comp audit, and your insurance costs. One question that comes up often: workers compensation appears here in your burden rate and again in the overhead section of Tool

#5. That is not double-counting. Your burden rate captures the workers comp premium tied to field labor — the portion calculated on your field payroll and applied to job costs. The overhead line in Tool #5 captures any remaining workers comp costs not already absorbed through burden, such as coverage for office staff or any policy minimum charges. When you build your burden rate, use only the field labor portion. Your CPA or insurance broker can help you confirm how your policy premium is split between field and office.

Total Annual Burden Costs divided by Total Annual Field Labor Hours equals your Burden Rate Per Hour. Or as a percentage: Total Annual Burden Costs divided by Total Annual Base Wages equals your Burden Percentage.

Calculate it once. Apply it consistently. Review it every year when your insurance renews.

The Core Components of Effective Job Costing

To make this tool work you must have:

- Accurate original budgets entered before work begins
- Clean phase codes aligned consistently to accounting accounts
- Timely entry of all costs — not at month end but as they occur
- Labor burden applied to every hour of field labor
- Change orders integrated into the job budget when approved
- Monthly review of budget versus actual by phase

Without monthly review, job costing is just data entry. Review is where it becomes protection.

Case Example: The Busy Company

Real-World Scenario

A subcontractor runs multiple jobs at once. Revenue is high. Crews are working. The schedule is full. But job costing is loose. Labor is not coded by phase. Burden is not applied. Change orders are tracked in email, not financially. At year end, profit is 3% and the owner is exhausted. When strict job costing is implemented, two job types consistently underperform, one crew consistently overruns labor hours, and change orders are approved but not billed timely. Nothing changed operationally. Visibility changed. Within a year, margins improve to 9%.

Not from more work. From better measurement.

A Narrative Walkthrough: The Riverside Office Fit-Out

A commercial GC wins a tenant improvement project — an office fit-out for a professional services firm. The contract value is $380,000. The job is estimated to take four months. Before the first nail goes in, the controller sits down with the project manager and builds the budget by phase:

- Field Labor (phases 01, 06, 09): $85,000
- Labor Burden at 28%: $23,800
- Materials (phases 06, 09): $110,000
- Subcontractors — electrical and HVAC (phases 12, 13): $95,000
- Equipment Rental (phase 14): $12,000
- Permits and Fees (phase 01): $8,000
- Other — consumables and fuel (phase 01): $6,200

Total Estimated Job Cost: $340,000
Estimated Gross Profit: $40,000
Estimated Gross Margin: 10.5%

Not a fat margin. But the job was bid competitively and the owner wants the client relationship. The budget is tight and the controller knows it. That matters.

Month one closes. The controller pulls the job cost report by phase and compares to budget. Field Labor actual: $27,000 against a month-one budget of $21,250. That is $5,750 over in the first month — a 27% overrun. Materials are on track. Subcontractors have not mobilized yet. Everything else is clean.

The controller calls a meeting. Not an alarm. A conversation: I want to show you where the Riverside job is tracking on labor. We are 27% over in month one. Before we get deeper into the schedule I want to understand if this is a timing issue — maybe we front-loaded the crew — or if we have a productivity problem we need to address.

The project manager confirms: the crew hit unexpected existing conditions in the demo phase. Two extra days of labor, unplanned. The controller reviews the contract — this type of condition falls within the contractor's scope. There is no additional revenue. The cost is absorbed. The controller documents it, adjusts the total estimated cost upward by $5,750 to $345,750, and recalculates against the unchanged contract value of $380,000. Revised estimated gross margin: 9.0%. Still acceptable. Crisis avoided. And the controller knows exactly where the job stands — because they were watching in month one.

But only because the controller was watching in month one — not month four.

Job costing does not just record what happened. It tells you where you are going while you still have time to steer.

How This Builds the Business Stronger

When job costing is disciplined, underbidding is corrected over time because you can see where estimates consistently miss. Strong crews are identified and deployed strategically. Weak processes are exposed before they become patterns. Pricing becomes grounded in real data instead of optimism. Change order discipline improves because the cost impact is visible immediately. Gross margin stabilizes because the leaks are found and fixed.

Controller Action Steps

Download the free Excel worksheets at www.constructionaccountantstoolbox.com.

1. Set up your standard phase code list and distribute it to every project manager and field supervisor before the next job starts.

2. Ensure every job has a finalized budget entered by phase before production begins.
3. Confirm field labor is coded by phase — not lumped into one account.
4. Calculate your burden rate and apply it consistently to every job budget.
5. Require documented change orders before execution and integrate them into the job budget when approved.
6. Review job cost reports by phase every month — not at closeout.

Measurement is not punishment. It is protection.

Tool #3

Work in Progress (WIP): The Oxygen of Construction

If job costing tells you how a job is performing, WIP tells you whether the company can breathe.

In construction, revenue does not move evenly. Costs do not move evenly. Cash does not move evenly. But financial statements often pretend that they do. WIP corrects that distortion. Without it you are guessing. With it you are managing.

What WIP Is and Why It Matters

Work in Progress is the structured comparison of costs incurred to date, estimated total costs, contract value, revenue earned to date, and amount billed to date. From this comparison you determine whether each job is overbilled or underbilled, what revenue has truly been earned, and what gross profit is real versus what is a timing illusion.

Without WIP the income statement may look strong. With WIP you may discover a job is overbilled and future cash is already spent, a job is underbilled and cash strain is coming, estimated costs were inaccurate, or gross profit is overstated. It removes illusion. And illusion is comfortable — right up until it is catastrophic.

A Note on Terminology

Under current GAAP standards — specifically ASC 606, which governs revenue recognition — the governing standard changed, but the underlying method did not. The cost-to-cost calculation you will learn in this tool is the same one construction companies have always used. ASC 606 updated the language: what was called "percentage of completion" is now described as recognizing revenue "over time" using the cost-to-cost input method. Your CPA may use either term — they mean the same thing. Contract assets and contract liabilities are the updated balance sheet labels for what used to be called underbillings and overbillings. This book uses plain construction industry terms throughout, with the technical equivalents noted where it matters.

The Mechanics

Every month, calculate the following for each active job:

- Percentage Complete = Costs Incurred to Date divided by Estimated Total Cost
- Revenue Earned to Date = Percentage Complete multiplied by Contract Value
- Compare Earned Revenue to Amount Billed

If Earned is greater than Billed — the job is underbilled. You have performed more work than you have invoiced. This is a contract asset on your balance sheet and a signal to get a billing out immediately.

If Billed is greater than Earned — the job is overbilled. You have invoiced more than you have earned based on actual progress. This is a contract liability on your balance sheet. In plain terms: it is money you have collected for work you have not yet done. It must be protected — not spent.

One important technical point: materials that have been purchased and delivered to a job site but not yet installed do not count toward your percentage complete. If you have $40,000 in materials sitting in a storage container at the site, those materials represent future work — not completed work. Including them in your cost-to-date would overstate your percentage complete and make your margin look stronger than it is. Confirm with your project manager what has actually been installed versus what is staged.

Case Example: The Overbilling Trap

Real-World Scenario

A GC has multiple overbilled jobs. The income statement looks healthy. Cash in the bank looks strong. The owner takes distributions. Six months later projects enter heavy cost phases. Bills exceed incoming draws. Cash tightens. Stress rises. The company was not profitable. It was living on advanced billing. WIP would have shown that — and a disciplined controller would have protected that cash.

Case Example: The Underbilling Problem

Real-World Scenario

A subcontractor consistently underbills. The owner does not want to upset the GC. Billing lags production. The company is technically profitable but constantly short on cash. The owner believes margins are weak. In reality, billing discipline is weak. WIP exposes this — and the fix is a billing submission, not a margin adjustment.

Running the Numbers: The Riverside Job at Month Two

Using the Riverside project from Tool #2, here is what the WIP schedule shows at the end of month two:

- Contract Value: $380,000
- Estimated Total Cost: $345,750 (revised after change order)
- Costs Incurred to Date: $155,588
- Amount Billed to Date: $190,000

Step one — Percentage Complete: $155,588 divided by $345,750 equals 45%.

Step two — Revenue Earned to Date: 45% multiplied by $380,000 equals $171,000.

Step three — Compare: Billed $190,000 versus Earned $171,000. The company is overbilled by $19,000.

That $19,000 is a contract liability on the balance sheet. It is not profit. It is not free cash. It is money collected for work not yet performed. If the owner takes a distribution based on what the bank balance shows, the company will feel real cash pressure in months three and four when costs accelerate and billing has nowhere left to go.

Now imagine the controller has eight jobs running simultaneously. Some overbilled. Some underbilled. The WIP schedule combines all of them into a single picture of where the company truly stands — independent of what the bank balance says on any given day. That picture is what banks examine when reviewing your line of credit. What bonding companies use to assess your capacity. What tells the owner whether they are ahead of the work or behind it.

A clean monthly WIP schedule is one of the most powerful credibility tools a small construction company can have. It costs nothing to build except discipline and consistency.

How This Builds the Business Stronger

When WIP is disciplined, revenue recognition becomes accurate, banks trust your reporting because the numbers are verifiable, bonding capacity increases because underwriters can see your true position, distribution decisions become smarter because overbillings are identified and protected, and margin erosion is caught early rather than discovered at job closeout.

Controller Action Steps

Download the free Excel worksheets at www.constructionaccountantstoolbox.com.

1. Build a WIP schedule for every active job — monthly without exception.

2. Confirm with project managers which materials are installed versus staged before calculating percentage complete.
3. Reconcile WIP results to your general ledger every close.
4. Identify underbillings immediately and submit billings before the next draw cycle.
5. Protect overbilled cash — flag it clearly to ownership as a contract liability, not available income.
6. Tie WIP results into your cash flow forecast every month.

Tool #4

Construction Cash Flow: Survival vs. Strength

Profit is theory. Cash is reality.

You can show profit on a job and still miss payroll. You can look strong on paper and still be one delayed draw away from panic. Construction cash flow is not normal business cash flow. It moves in waves. And if you do not understand the timing of those waves, growth becomes dangerous.

What This Tool Is

Construction cash flow is the management of billing timing, draw schedules, retainage, vendor terms, payroll cycles, overhead obligations, and project phase timing. It is not about how much money you make. It is about when money moves — and whether you can survive the gaps.

Why Small Construction Companies Struggle

Because they confuse revenue with liquidity. They assume that if they are busy they are fine. Busy companies fail every year — not from lack of work but from lack of cash discipline. Common mistakes include taking distributions during overbilling cycles, ignoring retainage buildup, not forecasting draw timing, paying vendors faster than collecting from clients, and expanding overhead before stabilizing margin.

Cash does not forgive optimism.

The Full Picture: How Cash Moves Through a Job

To truly understand construction cash flow you have to follow the money from the first billing to the last dollar collected. The beginning and the end of a job create completely different cash dynamics.

At the start, costs hit immediately. Materials must be purchased before work begins. Subcontractors mobilize and expect payment. Your field crew is on site and payroll runs every week regardless of when the next draw arrives. This is why front-loading billing — billing more heavily in the early phases to recover material and mobilization costs — is a common and legitimate practice. If you need $80,000 in materials on site before the first wall goes up, you cannot wait for the billing cycle to catch up.

But what you bill early is not profit. It is working capital protection. The controller must track it on the WIP schedule as a contract liability — not as earned income available for distribution.

Throughout the life of the job the payment cycle creates a structural gap. You complete work today but may not receive payment for 30 to 60 days after billing. Payroll does not wait. Materials do not wait. Your overhead does not wait. This gap exists on every draw, every month, for the life of the project. The bigger the project the bigger the gap between when costs are incurred and when payments arrive.

Retainage: The Cash You Earned but Cannot Touch

Retainage is silent pressure. On most commercial jobs and multi-home contracts, the client or GC holds 10% of each progress payment throughout the life of the project. That money has been earned. It appears on your WIP schedule as retainage receivable — a genuine asset on your balance sheet, money owed to you. But it is not in your bank account. You cannot touch it until the job is 100% complete and accepted.

On a $1,000,000 commercial job the client is holding $100,000 of your money.

That is not a theoretical number. That is cash your company has earned but cannot access. A disciplined controller tracks total retainage outstanding by job, ages it, monitors anticipated release dates, and flags any retainage that is past expected payment terms.

Retainage owed to you is an asset — recorded as retainage receivable or as a contract asset on your balance sheet depending on whether conditions for release remain. It is not income until collected, and it must be tracked separately from your regular accounts receivable so you always have a clear picture of what is outstanding and when it is expected.

The End-of-Job Decision: Change Orders and the Retainage Trap

As a job approaches completion — say 95% to 98% complete on the WIP schedule — a specific decision gets made that most people do not recognize as a financial decision.

The job is nearly done. Punch list is manageable. Retainage billing is almost in sight. And then the client says: while you are here, can we add a few items? We will make it a change order. It feels like found money.

But here is what actually happens financially. That change order extends the job. The punch list grows because now there is new scope. The client has new leverage — they can hold your retainage until the change order work is also complete and accepted. Your $100,000 in retainage, which was weeks away from being billed and collected, is now tied to additional work that may take weeks more to complete, inspect, and approve.

And once the retainage billing is finally submitted, the payment clock starts again — another 30 to 60 days depending on contract terms and client history.

Do the math. A few thousand dollars in change order revenue. Weeks of additional crew time on site with labor and overhead running. $100,000 in retainage sitting uncollected for an additional 60 to 90 days. The interest cost on a line of credit during that period is real. The opportunity cost of crew and equipment time is real. The cost of keeping a superintendent managing a nearly finished job instead of starting the next one is real.

The fastest way off a job is almost always the most profitable way off a job.

When a late change order conversation comes up on a job approaching retainage billing, the controller's job is to put one question in front of the owner clearly and without emotion: is this additional revenue worth the cost of what we are giving up to earn it? Sometimes yes. A substantial change order with strong margin on a client relationship worth protecting is a different calculation than a small scope addition that delays $100,000 in retainage for two months. But it must be a calculation — not a reflex.

The Hidden Cost of Working Past Your Billing Window

The controller's job is to see this before it happens. A consistent pattern of underbilling, or a billing schedule that lags production by more than one draw cycle, is a warning sign that the company is borrowing against its own retainage. The 90-day cash forecast will reveal this — but only if underbillings and retainage balances are both tracked and reconciled monthly. When the forecast shows that retainage release is the plan for covering a future cash shortfall, that is not a plan. That is a problem that needs to be addressed now, at the billing level, before the company reaches the end of the job with nothing left in the well.

The Monthly Cash Forecast

Every small construction company should maintain a rolling 90-day cash projection. Not complex. Just disciplined. Include expected draw receipts by job, anticipated retainage releases, payroll cycles, vendor payments due, overhead obligations, and any loan or line of credit payments. This forecast — updated at the beginning of every month — is what prevents reactionary decision-making. It allows planning instead of panic.

Case Example: Growth That Broke the Company

Real-World Scenario

A GC lands two large projects at once. Revenue doubles. Excitement builds. They hire staff, upgrade equipment, expand office space. But both projects require heavy upfront labor and materials before the first major draw. Cash dips hard. The line of credit maxes out. Stress explodes. The jobs were profitable. The timing was lethal. A 90-day cash forecast built before the expansion decision would have shown exactly what was coming.

How This Builds the Business Stronger

When cash flow is managed strategically, payroll is predictable, vendors respect you, banks trust you because your cash position never surprises them, growth decisions are made against a real forecast instead of a feeling, and the owner stops making distribution decisions based on the bank balance alone.

Controller Action Steps

Download the free Excel worksheets at www.constructionaccountantstoolbox.com.

1. Build a rolling 90-day cash forecast and update it at the start of every month.
2. Track total retainage outstanding by job with expected release dates.
3. Align billing timing with actual cost progress — do not let billing lag production.
4. Protect overbilled cash from distribution — flag it as a contract liability every month.
5. Before approving a late-stage change order, calculate the true cost of delayed retainage release.
6. Communicate cash trends to ownership early — never let them be surprised by a shortfall you saw coming.

Cash management is not fear-based. It is strength-based.

Tool #5

Overhead Allocation: The Margin Multiplier

Most small construction companies know their revenue. Some know their gross profit. Very few truly understand their overhead. And almost none allocate it intentionally.

Overhead is not just the cost of doing business. It is the weight your company carries every month — whether you build one job or ten. If you do not measure it properly, you cannot price properly. If you cannot price properly, margin becomes accidental.

What This Tool Is

In the three-tier COA structure built in Tool #1, overhead lives in the 7000 section of the general ledger — true company-wide costs that exist regardless of how many jobs are running or how many divisions are active. Overhead allocation is the discipline of understanding that monthly cost load, calculating the break-even revenue the company must generate to cover it, and determining what portion of those costs can be reasonably assigned to departments based on their activity.

Not all overhead can be allocated to departments or projects. Legal fees, marketing expenses, and executive compensation not tied to project management are general and administrative costs that belong to the company as a whole. They stay in the 7000 section of the general ledger and are absorbed at the company level. What can be allocated — certain insurance components, supervision costs that benefit multiple divisions, equipment depreciation tied to division activity — flows proportionally to departments based on revenue or labor hours.

How much must we earn — before profit even begins?

What Can and Cannot Be Allocated to Projects

This distinction matters for your financial reporting, for your bonding company, and for the integrity of your job costing. Under GAAP, specifically ASC 606 and ASC 340-40, costs can only be allocated to projects if they directly relate to fulfilling that contract.

Costs that CAN be allocated to projects:

- Field supervision and project management salaries — time spent managing active jobs
- Workers compensation insurance — directly tied to field payroll on specific jobs
- Builder's risk insurance — when written for a specific project
- Equipment depreciation — for tools used directly on job sites
- Field vehicle expenses — with documented job-site usage logs

Costs that CANNOT be allocated to projects:

- Legal fees — including contract drafting and general counsel
- Marketing and advertising expenses
- Executive and owner compensation not tied to project management
- General office rent
- CPA and accounting fees
- Company-wide general liability insurance — the G&A portion
- Software subscriptions for general business use

- Business development costs for work not yet won

The clearest test: would this cost exist if we had no active projects this month? If yes — it belongs in the 7000 section of the general ledger and stays out of project allocation. When you allocate costs that should not be allocated, you distort your job margin reporting and misrepresent the true cost of completing a contract. Banks and bonding companies trained to review WIP schedules will notice.

The Break-Even Reality

Every construction company has a monthly break-even number. If overhead is $150,000 per month and your average gross margin is 25%, you must generate $600,000 in revenue just to cover overhead — before one dollar of profit. Most small companies have never calculated this number. They bid emotionally. They grow revenue without understanding their operating load. And then wonder why profit feels thin.

Running Your Break-Even: A Narrative Walkthrough

Pull up your P&L. Go to the 7000 section of the general ledger. Write down every line item that exists whether you build one job or ten. For a typical commercial GC in the three-to-eight-million-dollar revenue range, that list looks something like this:

- Office Payroll — admin and controller: $18,000 per month
- Owner Salary — operating portion: $12,000 per month
- Rent and Utilities: $4,200 per month
- Insurance package — general liability, inland marine, auto: $5,800 per month
- Workers Compensation Insurance (monthly amortization): $3,500 per month
- Vehicle Expenses — non-job specific: $2,100 per month

- Software and Technology: $1,400 per month
- Marketing and Business Development: $1,000 per month
- Professional Fees — CPA and legal: $1,500 per month
- Miscellaneous Administrative: $800 per month

Total Monthly Overhead: $50,300

That is what it costs this company to exist — before one dollar of job cost, before one hour of field labor, before one board of lumber. Note that workers compensation is listed separately from the GL/Inland Marine/Auto package because it renews independently and its premium is calculated on payroll rather than revenue. The workers comp amount listed here represents the office-staff and policy-minimum portion — the field-labor portion of the workers comp premium is already absorbed through the burden rate applied to job costs (see Tool #2).

Now pull your average gross margin from the last 12 months. For this example, 22%.

Break-Even Formula: Monthly Overhead divided by Gross Margin Percentage.

$50,300 divided by 0.22 equals $228,636 per month.

That is the number. The company must generate $228,636 in revenue every single month just to cover overhead and break even. Not to profit. Not to grow. Just to exist. Now ask yourself: does the owner know that number? In most small construction companies the answer is no.

When you bring that number to an ownership meeting — clearly, calmly, with the math behind it — something shifts. Decisions about taking on a smaller job, adding an admin person, or expanding office space now have a reference point. The owner is no longer deciding by feel. They are deciding against a baseline.

The break-even number is not a one-time calculation. It is a living benchmark. Update it quarterly.

Department Allocation: Seeing What Each Division Actually Costs

Once you know your total monthly overhead, you can allocate the allocatable portion to departments proportionally. The simplest method: if Commercial generates 60% of total company revenue, it absorbs 60% of allocatable overhead. Residential generates 40%, it absorbs 40%. This allocation goes through the 6000 accounts as a departmental charge, making each division's P&L reflect the true cost of running that division.

When this is done correctly, department P&Ls become honest. And honest reporting drives real decisions.

Case Example: The Profitable Division

Real-World Scenario

A company runs Commercial and Residential divisions. Commercial shows strong gross margins. Residential looks weaker. But overhead is not allocated by division. When overhead is proportionally allocated, Commercial carries 70% of overhead and Residential carries 30%. After allocation, Residential is actually more efficient per dollar of overhead absorbed. Without allocation, the owner was protecting the wrong division.

The Hidden Danger of Growth

When revenue increases, owners often add office staff, vehicles, software, office space, and layers of management. Overhead grows faster than margin. Revenue doubles. Net profit barely moves. Because overhead was not measured before expansion. Bringing the break-even number to every expansion conversation is how the controller protects the company from growing into financial strain.

How This Builds the Business Stronger

When overhead is measured, allocated, and shared with ownership consistently, pricing becomes grounded in real cost recovery, division performance becomes visible and actionable, hiring and expansion decisions are made against a known baseline, and profit stops being accidental. Overhead clarity is financial maturity.

Controller Action Steps

Download the free Excel worksheets at www.constructionaccountantstoolbox.com.

1. Calculate your total monthly overhead in the 7000 section of the general ledger — every line item without exception.
2. Calculate your break-even revenue number and present it to ownership at your next monthly meeting.
3. Identify which overhead costs are allocatable to departments and which are company-level G&A.
4. Allocate the allocatable portion to divisions proportionally by revenue or labor hours — at minimum quarterly.
5. Compare overhead growth to revenue growth annually — flag any quarter where overhead is growing faster.
6. Ensure your pricing model includes overhead recovery on every bid.

Tool #6

Internal Controls: Protecting the Structure

You do not need a massive accounting department to have strong internal controls. You need consistency.

Internal controls sound intimidating. They are not. They are structure. And structure is something any disciplined person can build. Internal controls protect cash, profit, reputation, trust — and you. If you are conscientious and willing to learn, you absolutely can build this.

What Internal Controls Are

Internal controls are the systems that ensure transactions are accurate, payments are authorized, changes are documented, access is restricted appropriately, errors are corrected quickly, and fraud risk is reduced. They create reliability. And reliability builds confidence — with owners, banks, bonding companies, and vendors.

Controls are not about suspicion. They are about stability. Most small companies run on speed and relationships. But speed without structure creates mistakes. And mistakes compound.

The Minimum Standard

Even a small construction company should have:

- Separation between bill entry and check signing where possible
- Owner approval thresholds for payments above a defined amount
- Monthly bank reconciliations completed and reviewed — no exceptions
- Restricted access to editing paid transactions
- Documented change order approval process in writing
- Payroll review and approval before final submission
- Journal entry review discipline — no entry posts without review

None of this requires advanced education. It requires attention. And you are capable of attention.

Insurance: What It Is, How It Works, and Why the Accounting Matters

Insurance in a construction company is not a simple expense. It is a structured financial obligation that requires specific accounting treatment.

Most small construction companies carry their core insurance coverages in a single package: general liability, inland marine, and commercial auto. These are typically bundled together by your broker for a premium discount. The general liability premium is based on your gross revenue — the carrier will ask for your projected annual sales at renewal and that number determines your premium. The inland marine policy covers your equipment — tools, machinery, and gear — whether on a job site, in transit, or in storage. Auto covers your company vehicles.

Workers compensation is typically a separate policy. That premium is based on your total payroll broken down by employee classification codes. A project manager carries a very different rate than a roofer on a commercial job site.

Both policies — the package and the workers comp — renew annually and are typically paid upfront as a lump sum or in installments.

The Accounting Treatment:

When you pay an annual premium upfront, that payment does not hit the expense account all at once. It goes into a prepaid insurance account on the balance sheet first. Then every month a journal entry moves one-twelfth of the annual premium out of prepaid and into the appropriate 7000 overhead expense account. This matches the expense to the period it covers and prevents the distortion of a massive insurance expense in one month and nothing for the remaining eleven.

The journal entry is simple:

- Debit: Insurance Expense (7000 section of the general ledger) — one month's portion
- Credit: Prepaid Insurance (balance sheet) — same amount

Do this every month without exception. It is one of the most important recurring entries in the monthly close.

Critical: update your accrual rates every time your policy renews. Your workers comp and general liability premiums change at renewal based on payroll, revenue, claims history, and classification codes. If you set up your monthly accrual rate in January and your policy renews in July at a different premium, every month from July forward is accruing at the wrong rate. By year end the difference can be material. When your renewal package arrives, recalculate your monthly accrual rate that same week and update your journal entry template.

Subcontractor Compliance: This Is Not Optional

Before any subcontractor performs a single hour of work for your company, you need a complete subcontractor packet on file. Not after they start. Before. Get this wrong and it will cost the company real money.

The subcontractor packet must include:

- A completed W-9 with their legal business name, address, and EIN — for

year-end 1099 issuance
- A current certificate of insurance showing active general liability coverage
- A current certificate of insurance showing active workers compensation coverage
- A signed subcontractor agreement including your invoice format requirements and minimum insurance limits

If they cannot provide both certificates before work begins — they do not work for you. That is not a preference. That is a policy.

The Annual Workers Comp Audit Exposure

Every year your workers compensation policy goes through a premium audit. The auditor will review your financials and ask for certificates of insurance for every subcontractor you paid during the policy period. If a subcontractor paid during the year does not have a valid certificate on file, the payments you made to them will be reclassified as your own payroll — and your premium will be recalculated accordingly at whatever classification code rate applies to that type of work. On a high-risk trade that recalculation can be significant.

This is not a theoretical risk. It happens every year to small construction companies that did not track certificates carefully.

One additional detail that protects you at audit: require every subcontractor to separate labor and materials on their invoices. If a subcontractor is found to be uninsured, the auditor applies the classification code rates only to the labor portion — not to materials. If the invoice does not separate them, the auditor estimates the split — and that estimate will not favor you.

The Lapse Problem

A certificate of insurance is valid on the day it is issued. It does not guarantee coverage for the full year. Subcontractors — especially smaller ones — let their coverage lapse. They miss a payment. Their carrier cancels. And they keep working because nobody checked.

Verify coverage on your state workers compensation board website before releasing payment each week. Most states have a public lookup tool where you enter the subcontractor's EIN and confirm their coverage is active. Log the verification date in your records. If coverage has lapsed, hold payment and notify the owner immediately.

This weekly step takes minutes. Discovering at audit that three subcontractors let their coverage lapse during the year can cost thousands.

Case Example: The Permission Issue

Real-World Scenario

An AP clerk has permission to edit paid invoices. A check number is changed accidentally. A duplicate payment slips through. Vendor confusion begins. No fraud — just weak controls. When permissions are tightened and a review step is added, errors drop immediately. One control. One review step. The problem disappears.

Case Example: Payroll Mapping Mistake

Real-World Scenario

Payroll burden is not mapped correctly to job cost. Labor cost appears lower than reality for months. Bids are built on distorted data. Once mapping is corrected, future pricing improves. Internal control is not only about catching theft. It is about catching distortion.

How This Builds the Business Stronger

When internal controls are consistent, errors decrease, financial reports become trustworthy, owner confidence grows, outside advisors respect your reporting, and the company moves from reactive clean-up to proactive leadership. You stop fixing problems after they happen. You start preventing them.

Controller Action Steps

Download the free Excel worksheets at www.constructionaccountantstoolbox.com.

1. Review user permissions in your accounting system — who can edit paid transactions?
2. Ensure bank reconciliations are completed monthly without exception.
3. Establish and document payment approval thresholds with ownership.
4. Build your subcontractor onboarding packet and require it before the first day of work.
5. Verify subcontractor insurance coverage on the state website before every payment run.
6. Update your insurance accrual rates every time a policy renews.
7. Create a monthly close checklist and complete it in the same order every month.

You do not need a degree to do this. You need discipline. And if you have made it this far in this book, you already have that.

Tool #7

Financial Interpretation: Turning Numbers Into Decisions

Here is where everything changes. Not because the work gets harder. Because the purpose gets bigger.

Up to this point you have been building structure — Chart of Accounts, Job Costing, WIP, Cash Flow, Overhead, Controls. That is the foundation. But a foundation is not a building.

What you do with that foundation — how you read it, explain it, and act on it — that is where you become more than a bookkeeper. That is where you become a builder.

What Financial Interpretation Is

Financial interpretation is the ability to look at a report and understand what it is saying, what it is not saying, what it means for the business, what the owner needs to know, and what action should follow. It is the bridge between data and decision. And in small construction companies that bridge is almost always missing — not because the reports are wrong, but because no one is translating them.

You Can Learn This

Financial interpretation is not a gift. It is a skill. And like every skill in this book it is built through practice, curiosity, and consistency. You do not need years of experience to start asking better questions. You need the habit of asking them. Start here:

- What changed from last month — and why?
- Is gross margin holding or sliding?
- Which jobs are performing and which are not?
- Is overhead growing faster than revenue?
- Where is cash going that does not show up in profit?

Those are not advanced accounting questions. They are disciplined observation. And you are capable of both.

The Owner's Real Need

Most construction owners do not want a financial report. They want three things: are we making money, do we have enough cash, and are we safe to keep growing. Your job is to answer those three questions clearly every single month. Not with a stack of reports. Not with accounting jargon. With clarity. One page if possible. Plain language always.

Case Example: The Report Nobody Read

Real-World Scenario

A controller produces monthly financials — P&L, balance sheet, job cost summary. They are accurate. The owner glances at them and moves on. Nothing changes. When the controller shifts to summarizing three key points in plain language before presenting reports, the owner engages. Questions get asked. A margin problem surfaces. A pricing adjustment gets made. The reports did not change. The communication did. Interpretation creates action.

Case Example: The Sliding Margin Nobody Noticed

Real-World Scenario

A company's revenue grows 20% year over year. Everyone feels strong. But gross margin quietly slides from 28% to 21% over 18 months. No one flags it because dollar amounts look bigger. A controller who interprets — not just reports — catches the percentage trend. The conversation happens. Labor inefficiency is identified. Pricing is adjusted. Margin recovers.

Revenue growth without margin awareness is a slow leak. Interpretation catches it before it becomes a crisis.

What To Watch Every Month

You do not need to analyze everything. Watch these six data points consistently and you will catch most problems before they become serious:

- Gross margin percentage — is it holding month over month?
- Overhead as a percentage of revenue — is it growing?
- Top five jobs by cost — are they tracking to budget by phase?
- Cash position versus last month — what specifically moved it?
- Underbillings — are they growing without a corresponding billing in process?
- Owner draws versus net income — is the company being drained faster than it is earning?

The Language of Leadership

When you can walk into an owner meeting and say: gross margin held at 24% this month. Cash is down because we front-loaded labor on a large project before the first draw. Underbillings increased slightly — we need to push a billing this week. Overall we are on track.

That is not accounting. That is leadership.

The owner who hears that summary in plain language makes better decisions than the owner who looks at a P&L and sees complexity. You are the one who makes that clarity possible.

How This Builds the Business Stronger

When financial interpretation becomes a monthly discipline, problems surface early enough to fix, opportunities become visible before they close, owners make decisions with confidence instead of instinct, growth becomes intentional rather than reactive, and the controller becomes genuinely indispensable — not because of the reports they produce but because of the clarity they create.

Controller Action Steps

Download the free Excel worksheets at www.constructionaccountantstoolbox.com.

1. Before every owner meeting, write three to five plain-language sentences summarizing the financial position — no jargon.
2. Track gross margin percentage every month as a percentage, not just in dollars.
3. Flag any metric that moved more than 5% from prior month and know why before the meeting.
4. Connect cash movement to specific operational activity — draws received, payroll timing, retainage released.
5. Compare this month to the same month last year for context.
6. Ask yourself before every owner meeting: what does this person need to understand today to make a better decision tomorrow?

You are not just reporting history. You are informing the future.

Tool #8

The Owner Relationship: Building Trust Through Clarity

Everything in this book has been building to this. Not the reports. Not the reconciliations. Not the job cost summaries.

The relationship between the controller and the owner is the engine of financial strength in a small construction company.

When it works the company grows with intention. When it breaks down even perfect accounting becomes useless. Because information without trust goes nowhere.

What This Relationship Requires

The owner relationship is not a soft skill add-on. It is a strategic function. It requires communicating clearly, translating financial reality without alarm or sugarcoating, educating without condescending, protecting the business even when it creates friction, and earning the trust that allows hard conversations to happen. This is not about being liked. It is about being effective.

Why This Is Hard in Small Companies

In small construction companies the owner often built the company from nothing, carries enormous personal financial exposure, makes decisions on instinct and experience, and feels defensive about financial criticism. And the controller often feels uncertain about authority, avoids conflict to protect their position, holds back difficult information, and waits to be asked instead of leading. Both sides stay in their lane. And the company stays stuck.

The breakthrough happens when the controller decides to lead — not manage up, not wait for permission — but lead with clarity and care. You are not there to control decisions. You are there to make sure the right information is in the room when decisions are made. That is partnership.

Case Example: The Distribution Conversation

Real-World Scenario

An owner wants to take a significant distribution. Cash looks strong. But the controller knows two large projects are entering heavy cost phases next month, a draw is delayed, and retainage exposure is high. The easy path is silence. The right path is clarity: before we process this, I want to show you what cash looks like over the next 60 days. I want to make sure we are protected. That one conversation can prevent a cash crisis. That is not overstepping. That is exactly the job.

Case Example: Rebuilding Trust

Real-World Scenario

A controller inherits a company where the prior bookkeeper never challenged anything. The owner has learned to distrust financial reports and relies on gut feel and the bank balance. Rebuilding trust takes time — consistent accuracy, clear explanations, following through on every commitment, and never letting the owner be surprised by something the controller saw coming. Month by month, report by report, conversation by conversation, trust is rebuilt. And once it is there the owner starts asking questions instead of avoiding them. That transformation changes the company.

How To Communicate Financials to an Owner

Lead with the three answers every owner wants: are we profitable, are we safe on cash, is anything wrong that needs attention now. Then offer detail for anyone who wants to go deeper. Never lead with jargon. Never lead with volume of paper. If you cannot explain the financial position of the company in five minutes or less — simplify your summary, not your analysis. The analysis stays thorough. The communication stays clean.

Setting Limits With Confidence

Part of building a strong owner relationship is the ability to say difficult things. Not harshly. Not apologetically. Clearly. I do not think we should expand overhead right now — here is what I am seeing. This bid looks thin on labor — I want to walk through the numbers before we commit. The bank will ask about this when we renew the line — we should be prepared. A controller who only tells the owner what they want to hear is not a partner. They are a liability. You were hired to protect the company. Do that — with respect and consistency.

How This Builds the Business Stronger

When the owner and controller operate as genuine partners, decisions improve across the board, problems surface early enough to solve rather than survive, growth is planned rather than reactive, and the owner feels supported rather than alone in carrying the financial risk of the company. Most small construction companies have no one playing this role. You can be that person. And the impact over time is significant.

Controller Action Steps

Download the free Excel worksheets at www.constructionaccountantstoolbox.com.

1. Schedule a consistent monthly financial review with ownership — even 30 minutes makes a real difference.
2. Prepare a plain-language three-to-five-point summary before every meeting — no financial jargon.
3. Never let the owner be surprised by something you saw coming — speak early.
4. Bring a solution alongside every problem you raise.
5. Be consistent — trust is built through repetition, not through one brilliant moment.

6. Speak up early. Silence is not professionalism. It is avoidance.

Tool #9

Building a Company That Can Survive and Scale

This is where we talk about the finish line. Not retirement. Not exit. Not some distant future goal.

The finish line is a company that does not depend on any one person to survive.

Not the owner. Not the project manager. Not you. A company with structure strong enough to outlast individuals. That is the goal. And everything in this book has been moving toward it.

What Survivability Actually Looks Like

Building a survivable company means creating systems that function without heroics, financial reporting that speaks for itself, processes that transfer knowledge to the next person, structure that supports growth without chaos, and clarity that attracts banks, bonding, and opportunity. It is not about size. A five-million-dollar company can be built to last. A fifty-million-dollar company can be one bad year from collapse. The difference is not revenue. It is structure.

The Survivability Test

Ask these questions honestly:

- If the owner stepped away for 90 days, would the company function?

- If the controller left tomorrow, would the financial history be understandable to someone new?
- If the top project manager left, would job documentation support continuity?
- If the bank called today, could you produce clean financials within 48 hours?
- If a bonding company asked for three years of WIP schedules, could you deliver them?

Most small companies cannot answer yes to all five. That is not failure. That is the starting point. The goal is to work toward yes — intentionally, consistently, over time.

Case Example: The Company That Could Not Be Sold

Real-World Scenario

An owner builds a successful subcontracting company over 20 years — strong reputation, good revenue, loyal crew. When it is time to sell, the process stalls. Financial records are inconsistent. Job costing is incomplete. WIP schedules do not exist beyond the last two years. The company value lives in the owner's head, not in the systems. Buyers discount heavily or walk away. Twenty years of work undervalued because the structure was never built.

Financial discipline is not just about today. It is about what you are building toward.

Case Example: The Company That Survived a Crisis

Real-World Scenario

A mid-size contractor loses their top superintendent unexpectedly. It is a serious blow. But the company has documented job processes, strong financial reporting, clean WIP schedules, and a controller who understands every active project financially. They hire quickly. They transition smoothly. The work continues. Because the knowledge lived in the system — not just in the person.

Structure is resilience.

What Scalability Actually Requires

Scaling is not just growing revenue. Scaling is growing revenue without growing chaos proportionally. To do that you need financial systems that handle more volume without breaking, reporting that stays clean as complexity increases, overhead that grows intentionally not reactively, and a controller who grows with the company. That last point matters. You are not static. As the company scales your role scales. Your value increases with every system you build and every skill you develop. Protect that.

The Controller's Legacy

Here is something most accounting books never say: the work you do leaves a mark. When you build a clean Chart of Accounts, the next person who opens those books understands the company faster. When you document processes, the next controller serves the owner without starting from zero. When you maintain reliable WIP schedules, the bank sees a company that has been managed with discipline for years. When you establish strong internal controls, the company is protected even after you are gone.

You are not just doing a job.

You are building something that outlasts you.

That is legacy work.

The Owner's Responsibility

This book has been primarily addressed to the controller. But here is something for the owner reading these pages: your controller cannot build a strong company alone. They need your engagement with financial reporting, your willingness to have hard conversations, your discipline around distributions, your commitment to structure over shortcuts, and your trust in the process. The best controller in the world cannot protect a company whose owner resists financial discipline. This is a partnership. And the companies that build real strength — the ones that survive downturns, attract bonding, earn bank confidence, and create lasting value — those companies have owners and controllers who work together with honesty and intention.

How This Builds the Business Stronger

When a company is built to survive and scale, key person risk decreases, bank relationships strengthen, bonding capacity grows, company value increases for any future transition, owner stress decreases, and the team operates with the confidence that comes from knowing the systems work. The controller who helped build that — who built the systems, maintained the discipline, educated the owner, protected the cash, and showed up consistently — becomes something rare in small construction.

Trusted.
Indispensable.
Valuable.
Not because of a title.
Because of what they built.

Controller Action Steps

Download the free Excel worksheets at www.constructionaccountantstoolbox.co m.

1. Document your processes — if only you understand the system, the system is fragile.
2. Maintain consistent financial history — clean records compound in value over time.
3. Keep WIP discipline at a level that would hold up to bank or bonding scrutiny at any moment.
4. Grow intentionally — every new skill you develop strengthens your value to the company.
5. Have the survivability conversation with ownership. Ask the hard questions together.
6. Protect the structure you build. Do not let shortcuts erode what discipline created.

You started this book as someone who wanted to learn.
You finish it as someone who can build.
That is not a small shift.
That is the whole point.

The Non-Negotiable One Action Per Tool

IF YOU DO NOTHING ELSE

This book contains ten tools. Implementing all of them at once is not realistic and it is not the goal. The goal is to start. If you are overwhelmed, use this page. Pick one tool. Do the one thing listed for it. Then come back for the next one. Structure compounds. Every single improvement you make strengthens everything that follows.

Tool #1 — The Financial Blueprint

Separate your direct job costs, your department indirect costs, and your company overhead into three distinct sections of your chart of accounts. That structure is the foundation every other tool in this book is built on.

Tool #1B — The Balance Sheet Blueprint

Reconcile your bank account and post your WIP journal entries every single month without exception. Those two steps keep your balance sheet honest and your financial reporting real.

Tool #2 — Job Costing

Calculate your true labor burden rate using your actual payroll taxes, workers compensation, general liability, and PTO — and apply it to every job budget before the next bid goes out. "If your burden rate is not in your bids, your margin is already gone."

Tool #3 — WIP Schedule

Build a WIP schedule for every active job this month and present it to ownership. One month of honest WIP reporting will tell you more about your company's true financial position than a year of income statements.

Tool #4 — Cash Flow

Build a rolling 90-day cash forecast and update it at the start of every month. Write down every expected draw, every retainage release, every payroll cycle, and every overhead obligation. Cash does not forgive surprises.

Tool #5 — Overhead Allocation

Calculate your monthly break-even number — total overhead divided by your average gross margin — and bring it to your next ownership meeting. When the owner knows that number, every business decision changes.

Tool #6 — Internal Controls

Build your subcontractor onboarding packet and require it before the first day of work. W-9, general liability certificate, workers compensation certificate, signed agreement. No packet — no work. This one discipline protects you at every workers comp audit.

Tool #7 — Financial Interpretation

Before your next ownership meeting write three to five plain-language sentences summarizing the financial position. Are we profitable. Are we safe on cash. Is anything wrong that needs attention now. No jargon. No reports. Just clarity.

Tool #8 — The Owner Relationship

Speak up before the owner is surprised — not after. If you see a cash shortfall coming, a margin problem forming, or a distribution that should not happen right now, say it early. Silence is not professionalism. It is avoidance.

Tool #9 — Building to Scale

Document one process this month that only you understand. If the knowledge lives only in your head the system is fragile. Written processes protect the company, protect your work, and build the structure that lets the business outlast any one person.

You do not need to start with everything. You need to start.
Pick one. Build it right. Then the next one.

To the Person Who Started With Nothing

This chapter is not about accounting.

It is about you.

If you made it to this page, you are not the person who gives up when things get complicated. You are the person who leans in. And that matters more than any credential, any degree, or any title. The construction industry is full of talented people. Skilled builders. Hard workers. Dedicated owners. But it is short on people who combine financial discipline with genuine care for the business they serve.

That combination is rare. And you can be that person.

I Want to Tell You Something Directly

I did not start with all of this. I started with responsibility and a willingness to figure it out. I made mistakes. I fixed them. I inherited messes. I cleaned them up. I worked in companies that had no structure. And I built structure where there was none. Not because I had every answer. Because I kept asking better questions. That is available to you too. Right now. Where you are. With what you have.

What This Book Was Really About

On the surface this book was about Chart of Accounts, the Balance Sheet, job costing, WIP schedules, cash flow, overhead allocation, internal controls, financial interpretation, owner relationships, and scalability. But underneath all of it, this book was about one thing:

Giving small construction companies a fighting chance.

Most of them are run by people who are exceptional at building things. Roofs. Foundations. Electrical systems. Plumbing. Framing. Commercial interiors. They are craftspeople. And they deserve financial structure that matches their skill in the field. Most of them cannot afford a high-end advisory team. Most of them are working with limited capital and enormous personal risk. And most of them have someone in the office who is conscientious and capable and willing — but who has never been given the tools to do more than keep the books.

This book was written for that person. For you.

What Happens Next Is Up To You

You will not implement everything at once. You should not try. Pick one tool. Build it properly. Then pick the next one. Structure compounds. Every clean account code makes the next report more accurate. Every disciplined WIP schedule makes the next bank conversation easier. Every honest conversation with an owner builds trust that protects the company in the next difficult moment.

You are not building overnight. You are building consistently. And consistency is what creates lasting strength.

To the Owner Reading This

If you gave this book to someone on your team — or if you picked it up yourself because you knew something needed to change — hear this: financial strength is not just an accounting function. It is a leadership commitment. Your controller cannot protect what you are not willing to understand. But when you commit — when you engage with the numbers, trust the process, have the hard conversations, and build the structure — everything changes. You stop guessing. You start leading. And the company you built with your hands becomes something that can outlast you.

To the Controller Building Something Real

You are more valuable than you know. In an industry that moves fast and runs lean, the person who maintains discipline and builds clarity is the person who protects everything. You will not always get the credit. You will not always be in the room when the big decisions are made. But you will be the reason the company is still standing when others are not. You will be the reason the bank said yes. The reason the bonding came through. The reason payroll never missed. The reason the owner could sleep at night.

That is not a small contribution. That is the foundation everything else is built on.

A Final Word

Construction is one of the hardest industries in the world to run profitably. The margins are tight. The risk is real. The cash flow is unpredictable. The work is physical and demanding and relentless. And yet people build companies in this industry every single day. They take the risk. They hire the crews. They bid the jobs. They show up. The least you can do is give those companies the financial structure they deserve. Not because it is required. Because it is right.

Now go build something stronger.
You are ready.

www.ingramcontent.com/pod-product-compliance
Lightning Source LLC
LaVergne TN
LVHW011049110826
845149LV00015B/3426

* 9 7 9 8 9 9 5 9 4 8 2 1 6 *